DINOSAUR WORLD

Relatives of Dinosaurs

Robin Birch

CHELSEA
CLUBHOUSE

An Imprint of Chelsea House Publishers
A Haights Cross Communications ◆ Company
Philadelphia

This edition first published in 2003 in the United States of America by Chelsea Clubhouse, a division of Chelsea House Publishers and a subsidiary of Haights Cross Communications.

Chelsea Clubhouse
1974 Sproul Road, Suite 400
Broomall, PA 19008-0914

The Chelsea House world wide web address is www.chelseahouse.com

Library of Congress Cataloging-in-Publication Data

Birch, Robin.
  Relatives of dinosaurs / by Robin Birch.
  v. cm. — (Dinosaur world)

  Includes index.
  Contents: Dinosaurs — Reptiles — Pliosaurs — Plesiosaurs — Pterosaurs — A giant crocodile — A giant turtle — Names and their meanings.

  ISBN 0-7910-6991-5
  1. Animals, Fossil—Juvenile literature. [1. Prehistoric animals.] I. Title. II. Series.
  QE765 .B57 2003
  566—dc21

                                                                        2002000840

First published in 2002 by
MACMILLAN EDUCATION AUSTRALIA PTY LTD
627 Chapel Street, South Yarra, Australia, 3141

Copyright © Robin Birch 2002
Copyright in photographs © individual photographers as credited

Edited by Angelique Campbell-Muir
Illustrations by Nina Sanadze
Page layout by Nina Sanadze

Printed in China

Acknowledgements
Auscape/Jan Aldenhoven, p. 24, Auscape/Jean-Paul Ferrero, p. 29; Australian Picture Library/Corbis, pp. 17, 25; Corbis Digital Stock, p. 21; Kronosaurus, Museum of Comparative Zoology, Harvard Museum of Natural History; photo by Frank Siteman, © President and Fellows of Harvard College, p. 13; Getty Images/Photodisc, pp. 7 (top & bottom), 28; Southern Images/Silkstone, p. 6.

While every care has been taken to trace and acknowledge copyright, the publisher tenders their apologies for any accidental infringement where copyright has proved untraceable.

Contents

Dinosaurs

Dinosaurs lived millions of years ago. Some dinosaurs ate animals and others ate plants.

Some dinosaurs were big and some were small.

Reptiles

Reptiles are **cold-blooded** animals. They breathe air through their lungs, lay eggs, and have **scales** on their skin. Dinosaurs were reptiles.

Lizards and snakes are reptiles that live on Earth today.

7

Dinosaurs were reptiles that walked on land. They held their legs underneath their bodies, not out to the side as lizards do. There were no swimming or flying dinosaurs.

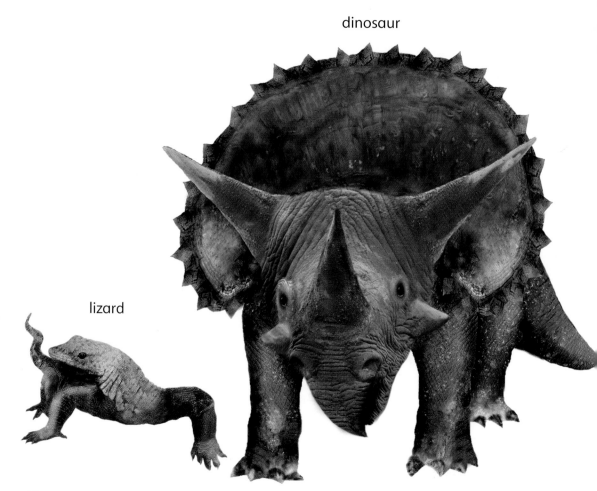

dinosaur

lizard

8

Many swimming and flying reptiles did live in the time of the dinosaurs. They were relatives of dinosaurs.

Pliosaurs

(PLEE-o-sawrs)

Pliosaurs were huge reptiles that lived in seas, lakes, and rivers. These swimmers ate other reptiles as well as fish and **shellfish**.

Pliosaurs had long heads. Long, sharp teeth filled their mouths. Their necks were short. They were very fierce **predators** and could catch any animal that lived in the water.

Pliosaurs had a tail and four big, strong flippers. They moved their flippers up and down to swim. Pliosaurs could swim very fast to catch their **prey**.

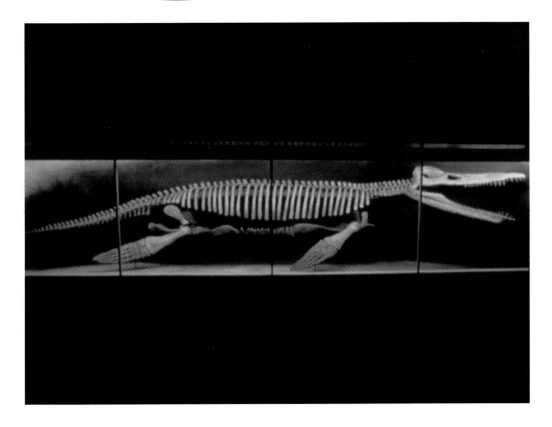

Scientists have dug up pliosaur bones to study. These **fossils** show us how pliosaurs looked.

Plesiosaurs

(PLES-ee-oh-sawrs)

Plesiosaurs were swimming reptiles that ate fish. They had small heads and sharp teeth. Their necks were very long.

Plesiosaurs had wide bodies, like turtles without shells. They had four flippers and a tail.

Plesiosaurs lived in seas, lakes, and rivers. Like other swimming reptiles, plesiosaurs came to the surface to breathe air.

Plesiosaurs could probably move on land by dragging themselves with their flippers, as turtles that live in water do today. They most likely laid eggs in nests in beach sand.

Pterosaurs

(TAIR-oh-sawrs)

Pterosaurs were flying reptiles. There were many different kinds of pterosaurs.

Pteranodon (tuh-RAN-uh-don) was one of the biggest pterosaurs. Its **wingspan** was about 25 feet (7.5 meters). Pteranodon had no teeth. It probably used its beak to scoop up fish from the sea.

The small pterosaur Rhamphorhynchus (RAM-for-INK-uhs) had sharp teeth to spear fish from the sea. It had a diamond-shaped flap of skin on its tail to keep it steady as it flew. Including its tail, Rhamphorhynchus was about 3 feet (1 meter) long. It had a wingspan of about 3 feet (1 meter).

Pterosaurs had good eyesight and were
excellent hunters. They dived into the sea
to catch fish as many sea birds do today.

A Giant Crocodile

Many types of crocodiles lived at the same time as the dinosaurs. They were very much like the crocodiles that live today.

The biggest known crocodile was Deinosuchus (DIE-noh-SOOK-uhs). It was a giant crocodile that measured 50 feet (15 meters) long. It lived in **swamps**, where it caught fish and small reptiles to eat.

Deinosuchus probably laid its eggs in nests, as crocodiles do today.

Crocodiles today carry their young in their mouths. Deinosuchus probably carried its young in the same way.

A Giant Turtle

Several kinds of turtles lived at the same time as the dinosaurs. One was a giant sea turtle called Archelon (ARK-uh-lahn).

Archelon was about 13 feet (4 meters) long. It had a wide, flat shell and a short tail. It moved its four paddle-shaped flippers up and down to swim in the sea.

Archelon had a narrow head with a beak that curved downward. It probably ate **jellyfish** as sea turtles do today.

Female Archelons laid their eggs in nests on sandy beaches. Newly hatched Archelons probably ran together to the sea in the same way that young sea turtles do today.

Names and Their Meanings

"Dinosaur" means "terrible lizard."

"Pliosaur" means "greater lizard."

"Plesiosaur" means "near lizard"; plesiosaurs were given this name because they were related to the dinosaurs.

"Pterosaur" means "winged lizard."

"Pteranodon" means "winged and toothless."

"Rhamphorhynchus" means "beak nose."

"Deinosuchus" means "terrible crocodile."

"Archelon" means "**ancient** turtle."

Glossary

ancient	from a very long time ago
cold-blooded	having a body temperature that is the same temperature as the surrounding air or water
fossil	something left behind by a plant or animal that has been preserved in the earth; examples are dinosaur bones and footprints.
jellyfish	a sea animal that has tentacles and a body that is soft like jelly
predator	an animal that hunts other animals for food
prey	an animal that is hunted by other animals for food
scales	small pieces of hard skin that cover the body of a reptile
shellfish	sea animals that live inside shells
swamp	an area of wet, spongy land
wingspan	the distance between the outer tips of an animal's wings

Index